Backwards Book Publishing

How to produce your books in reverse:
Save time, earn more income, and work less.

By Dr. Robert C. Worstell

With a collection of essays in alternative self-publishing
strategies and tactics.

Audio to these essays are as linked, along with
additional bonus downloads.

(PS. - Additional free downloads available in the back
of this book.)

Table of Contents

Bonus

Get No-Charge Access to Writing and Publishing Materials from Our Library Collection

Instant Access - Join Here

Click or type into your browser:

http://livesensical.com/go/writingbooks/

Publishing The Backwards Book

(Listen to the audio and/or watch the video here.)

The Scene You Face

The situation that most starting authors have (and I've seen the same thing you've run into) is: *How the hell do you get from here to there?*

You hear and (are constantly told) about these outrageously successful authors. But only a very small few percent of people actually achieve that.

If you want to be successful you've got to study success. What I found by studying all these guys that are making six- and seven-figures as an author is that most of them have been starting out with books and ending up with courses.

The beginning author, though, has to spend a lot of time and money they don't have in order to do that. So most authors fail to make a livable income.

And as if we don't have enough problems, how is it a solution to work *backwards*?

Book as an Idea Container

Let's go back to basics. *Books are an idea container.* They aren't just an e-book, a paperback, and so on. The one set of content is pushed out through all these different versions: e-books, paperbacks, hardbacks, audio books, audio CDs, and also -- *courses*.

The great part about that is courses sell the books and the books sell the courses.

Advantages to Courses

All these products tend to leverage each other. The advantages to courses is that they leverage existing content. You've already got this stuff there. So you just want to generate everything else out from it.

They also bring the audience from Amazon to you, rather than you pushing all your traffic to Amazon to get your sales. You actually are able to get these audience on to your mailing list and service them directly, and communicate with them personally. So you find out more and more about your audience and they get better service and better products from you. Eventually as they become superfans they then graduate into evangelists for your brand. They bring other people in as well. And all of this diversifies your income sources.

Difficulties in Making Courses

There's difficulties in making courses. First, they're video based primarily. And videos are very expensive in terms of time and money to produce any quality. For most courses they're on somebody else's platform so you have to drive traffic to them in order to make any sort of sales. Now, instead of being an author, you've turned into a full time marketer just to make money off this course. So courses don't usually get produced until last – if they do at all.

But the trick with courses is while an e-book is $3.99, a course that covers the same material as ebook is $299 or even $1000. So they can earn you the most money, the most income, fastest.

Conventional Sequence

For most book publishing: If you're going to do this route of all these products, you'd write, edit, proof, and publish all your text versions.

Then you'd turn around and either hire someone else or just personally record the audio, edit that audio, and then publish it as an audio book and audio CDs.

Then you turn around to get the course, You'd have to record the video, you have to edit and produce the course. A lot of people are doing: they create the presentation, record more audio for that presentation, and then do a screen capture or marry the slides to an audio recording.

And all of this is expensive both in time and money. So you can see why it seldom gets done.

Flaws

Now the flaws in the system, even on top of all we covered, is that most authors are working for Amazon as an employee without any benefits. Because, due to Amazon having these cliffs that they artificially generate at 30-60-90 day intervals. Most authors solve this by constantly writing more books. Every 30 days they have to come out with a new book, or maybe two months. And so that's just another job - "Just Over Broke."

And as a result of that, because you're so busy working on your books, if you're actually making money on your books you can get somebody hired out to do the audio, but the courses never get produced.

The highest-leveraged product you can have is a course and it will never get produced in most cases. Mainly, because there's too much time and cost, and also revisiting this old data one more time isn't as rewarding as writing a brand new book.

So what happens? You're leaving money on the table. Tons of it.

Better Way to Make A Course

A better way to make the course than what we've seen before in the conventional method is:

1. You do the research in outline you do for regular textbook that you're writing.

2. Then you create a PowerPoint from that outline.

3. Then you record the video live with screen capture.

4. You use the PowerPoint and you just talk over it.

5. Then you pull the audio out of that and have it transcribed.

6. And then you're able to create the course and publish all book versions at once.

So you leverage the sales on Amazon, and you also get extra sales outlets that are going to be pushing those courses for you.

Resources

You've got to look at your resources. What do you have to do this?

Ideally, a work-flow wouldn't cost you anything or very little in order to get going. Producing a text book is this way already: you've got your text editor, you just upload to Amazon, and you got a book. Well, you do have to make the cover.

But the other resource you also have is that you've already got a microphone. Most people have a web cam, or they work on a laptop which has a built in camera and a microphone. If you're doing podcasts, you already have a decent mic. Of course your Internet access is everywhere these days. You already have that at home and you're using this to produce your products anyway.

Of all of this, <u>transcribing</u> is the key hurdle that you need to jump.

Free Services

There are free services to do transcriptions. But as usual, you get what you pay for. YouTube will create transcripts for almost all videos. They use Google speech to text engine. The problem with these is you have no punctuation or capitalization in this stuff. And there some errors in this and some of those are very hilarious.

Your Chrome browser has sites and plug ins that will actually take advantage of that as long as you've got an Internet connection. They will actually generate this transcript for you using Google's speech text engine.

Apple also has a dictation engine built into their Macs. You just have to go down and turn it on. But again, you've got no punctuation or capitalization. You have to do a lot of editing to get even a first draft.

Paid Products

There are paid products out there. Most of these are all from Nuance - Dragon Naturally Speaking products. There's versions on the Mac, there's a version for Windows, through browsers, and even through your iPad.

But again these don't produce any punctuation or capitalization unless you specifically speak and tell them to. You have to pause and say "comma", and then you have to say "break" to get a paragraph break. You have to say "period" to get a period. You actually say "capital," and then the word, to capitalize the first word of that sentence.

Now if you're doing all this, it may distract you from your inspired performance. On top of that, you can't use that audio for the audio book or your video. And so you're going to have to record two versions. It costs you for the program and then it's going to cost you again in time to get this thing produced.

Paid Services

There are paid services to do this and you can find them really easily on the Internet. The average is a dollar a minute and it only takes a few days for them. You send them the file and they send you back the transcript. You can pay more to get it faster, of course. You can pay as much as 10 or 20 bucks per minute, to get it done the next day or overnight. The punctuation and capitalization is included. Of course for the better services, the more you want, the more you're going to have to pay.

Hybrid Services

I found a hybrid called Trint.com. It's only 25 cents a minute and you get a 30 minute free trial, if you want to try it out. You upload the audio and then the text shows up in the browser. I sent a five-minute file up there. And it was ready for me in less than two minutes.

Then I was able to edit the text right there in the browser. You could play the audio and correct the text as you go, without leaving the keyboard. It does includes the obvious punctuation and capitalization. There are some errors depending on how good the quality of your audio is. It's a big start. You can edit and finish your first draft online then download it as a word doc. And that's pretty pretty fascinating.

It's built on some fancy programming that they found, which is being used in the TV industry to provide transcripts for all the massive amounts of video that some of these news agencies produce.

Optimal Work Flow

Let's look at an optimal workflow then.

1. You would research your book as usual, outline and create a slide deck.

2. Then you record that slide deck with the screen capture.

3. Extract the audio from that.

4. You might want to edit that audio because you don't want to send up stuff with a bunch of goofs in it that you are then paying to get transcribed. But it's not vital.

5. Then they transcribe it for you.

6. Then that edited audio would immediately go right over into a podcast for promotion, or you could send it with the proper headings and you could actually create the chapters of your books. (You could edit it while you're waiting for the transcript...)

7. And send that up as an audio book or audio CDs. Now the video you're recording in one chunk is then cut down into shorter lessons. Of course you need to add headers and footers to these. The smart thing would be

to put those headers and footers into your slide deck and let them go through as you're recording.

8. From the transcript you can build course handouts from the text.

You can now publish the text, audio, and course versions all at the same time. And what that allows you to have the ebook, the paperback, and the hardback up there (if you want) which then makes the ebook look more valuable. Your readers can also buy the version that they most want to watch, or read, or listen to.

Promoting the Course

Your podcast uses the content that you just produced as audio to promote all these versions.

Your course is available and you have discount coupons in the backs of these e-books and hardcopy versions, so they can get a 50 percent discount off the Course. If they go to the back of the book and of course in your description for your book, you're saying, "Be sure to check out the back of the book for a special discount only for readers of this book."

You see how this leverages all possible ways, all possible things that you could possibly do? Of course you're going to get more visitors, more buyers, more income. This is what we're talking about.

- The books promote the courses with coupon in the back.

- The courses then sell the books as the course textbooks.

- You can then take the video and edit it into a webinar, by just adding the call to action.

- You're also then able to generate PDF handouts and post these up onto SlideShare, with links so that people can come right over to your books or right into your course.

- You can also nowadays embed short video clips right inside the SlideShare decks and they promote this so their viewers get it. Their viewers stay there and they'll watch your slide deck, because there's a four-minute video inside the slide deck, and it has all the data they need. Of course because the more time they spend on your site, then the more likely they are to buy. So you see how this just starts leveraging all the time...

- Of course then you can put up short video clips on YouTube promote all your products.

The Summary

My approach then would be this:

- Research and record.

- Extract the audio send it to Trint.com

- Edit it on Trint and download your first draft. We don't have to do all four drafts.

- Because your second draft puts in all the links and dresses it up.

- And the third draft is then your line edit.

- (Your fourth draft is usually where you speak it out loud, but that was done when you spoke it originally.)

- And then you get it proofed and then you're done.

That brings you into the usual route of book publishing, where then you take it and put up as e-book, paperback, and hardback.

Also then your audio would be ready, so you could have your audio book and audio CDs. Publish those as usual.

Meanwhile, you're compiling the course with all the different parts of it. And then you go live with everything at once.

Your Mileage May Vary

Now your mileage may very well vary. Because I tell everybody to test everything I tell you. Because there is no one-size-fits-all solution.

I found this in Launches. There are more ways to launch a book than Carter has pills-(to use an old phrase.) You have to find the setup that will work for you. I'm just telling you: "Here's another way you can try this. Check this out for yourself.

The main advantage of this approach is to publish all formats with less time in between. You'll see these authors do this: they'll put up their ebook, then they'll come back and put up their paperback, and that will help sales of their e-book. Then they'll hire somebody (and sometimes this is a year later) to do their audio book.

(Of course when we have an audiobook up there, that is one of hottest items to do right now. It will help raise your other book sales.)

But that's where they stop. The course usually never gets done, like I said.

The whole point is that you can get all this done, with less time in between. You can get everything simultaneously being launched. Huge launch. Because you have all these resources, then people will find out more and it will create a huge buzz and leverage all your sales.

The other thing is you're going to get your audience coming directly for you, more and more. They go on your list. They get in your course. You can communicate them. You can survey with them. You can find out what they want next, what they will want best, and you can produce more for them. The more you produce better, higher quality stuff, exactly what they want, then of course they're going to spend more with you. They become fans, superfans and evangelists. They can sell your courses and books for an affiliate commission. Really simple.

I can't say too much about how you have to test this for yourself, and try this out, and check it out.

I produced this for you after just a couple of days worth of research, as I thought you ought to have this right away.

May Your Income Rocket

I really do wish that you have every advantage to help your income rocket.

If have any questions go to http://LivingSensical.com

Leave a comment. And you can find my email and let me know.

OK? Thanks.

Does This Book Publishing Model Work?

(Listen to this audio here.)

This supplement is because I found I'd left something out of my slide deck. But also, I wanted to give you an update about this podcast you're listening to.

Eating my own dog food, I submitted the audio from the video I created over to Trint.com The initial count on the words is 3005. When I took out the time stamps and such, it came up as just over 2900. Total time on the video is 17:24. That means I'm talking about 170 words per minute. Amazon only needs 2500 words to publish as an ebook. This current text you are reading would add another thousand, giving us around 4,000 total. And that would give us about a 16-page ebook on its own. I would still need another 2,500 words in order to publish on CreateSpace. (I could probably get some unpublished essays around here, or include some popular podcasts.) So you can see the gears turning in my head here...

It should be an interesting journey of its own.

[**Update:** If you have this book in your hands or on your ereader, you've seen this become a reality.]

What was most interesting in editing the text was that my "writing" style changed. This stuff really sounds like I'm talking to you as if we're in the same room. Funny, isn't it?

The section I left out of the original mind map I started with was titled: "Does This Work?" (And I've included PDF's of that mindmap for download.)

The key part to this, is how does publishing backwards actually save time, work, to get more income?

I think I've beaten the leverage point about courses so you understand that courses will set you up with more diversified income sources, with those sources cross-recommending the other products and services you offer as an author.

But how does this save you time and effort?

Obviously, you don't have to do things twice or three times to get everything produced. And that means you can actually "go live" with all parts of this at once. That will help you with leveraging the maximal income from each type of product or service. (Courses are a service, books are products.)

The trick to saving you time is in how much faster spoken text is than writing.

A person on average talks at about 150 words per minute.

Now, when I type, I can get about 2,000 words out in an hour. Stephen King allots two hours to get that much. Some other how-to books set it at only 500 words per day to not overwhelm you. Chris Fox livened things up when he produced a book that showed people how to train themselves to write 5,000 words an hour.

But get this: talking is still faster. 150 words per minute is 9,000 words per hour.

And the way Chris Fox gets his speed is at the expense of typos and other errors you'd normally stop to correct. So you then have to come back to that same text to correct errors on a second day, which may bring you back down to the level of a 2,000 word author. But you're talking about the total time editing and producing a book, not how fast you can get the first draft done.

By recording and then transcribing your books, you produce them faster and so can publish more books each year, or spend time doing something else instead.

I'm a great fan of publishing short reads. These are books that are less than 100 pages and can be as short as 2500 words on Kindle. Short reads prove the genre to you and enable you to break into additional genres and markets. Instead of producing a huge book at 100,000 words, you publish ten 10,000-word books as both ebooks and thin paperbacks.

Instead of investing six months coming to market with your massive work, you are publishing every two weeks and building audience while you prove the market. You could be producing a major flop at those 100,000 words and have nothing to show for it. Or, if people don't like your first four books, then go ahead and publish the collection as a higher-priced ebook and paperback, and move to a nearby or completely different genre.

Publishing bi-monthly proves the market in just two months, and if you're writing good stuff, you are making income every month instead of living off savings. This is what E. L. James is doing right now, publishing a few chapters at a time of her next book and then improving these according to the feedback she gets. When all the chapters are complete, she'll publish the massive book, which will look like a bargain.

Now, most chapters are about 2,000 words long, so an hour and a half of transcriptions will bring that out for you.

Since we have a system described in that video which can have the transcript back to you the same day, you can get your 2nd and 3rd drafts done in another day, and then send it off for proofing. Create or meanwhile get someone to generate your cover, and you can have that ebook and POD paperback published by the end of the week.

You can be publishing a book a week, or 50 new books each year.

That's instead of two massive books which might not sell.

That's what speaking your book does for you. It speeds the whole scene up remarkably.

You've saved time and effort. And also made sure that you're going to get paid for your work.

Now, on a week's schedule, you're also going to have to get that course launched as well as the audio book. So that's probably the second week, meaning now we are down to "just" 25 books published in a year.

As I said in the video: books sell courses and courses sell books. So all your products will pitch the other books and services you offer. You've also added Udemy and Skillshare to the mix, so they are going to be pitching your courses and sending people to Amazon. Because there's a special discount offer in the back of the ebooks and paperbacks, Amazon will be sending people to your course and to your mailing list as well.

Now you're more productive, and have more income. What are you going to do with all that money and free time?

Something to think about.

And it all started when you decided to start publishing backwards from your course.

Check my math again. Test everything for yourself. Come up with a plan that works for you and your own resources. Then get really busy getting that plan done.

With all the existing authors we have, they are still not keeping up with the demand for new books. Meaning that there is still plenty of room for people who can crank out tons of content regularly.

Here's a chance for you to earn a bigger piece of that pie.

Good luck.

Keep me posted with your progress...

Note: The downloads I mentioned above are available here, along with the audio.

- - - -

Update

Overnight, I resolved to publish this as an ebook and paperback.

So I found and added some articles which have to do with the model of building books backwards from courses. As well, they are mostly very unique ways of self-publishing you haven't been hearing in all your studies.

At this writing the book is well over 13K words, enough to generate a 50+ page paperback.

All in less than 48 hours from idea to video to transcript, to podcast, to publishd book.

Since none of these articles have been seen in print before, it's a fair trade.

But no, this didn't mean I created a course out of these. And while I have audio for all these essays, it's not going to be an audiobook any time soon.

Because this book started out as a simple report while I was busy outlining a course I needed to build. Essentially, it's a preview of that course.

You will see a book show up which contains all the data of that course soon – but I have to get back to it.

Meanwhile, I've included the links to all the available audio in podcast format so you can download a version of this book to take with you where you would rather listen than read.

Otherwise, my podcast "<u>Selling Your Books Online</u>" is available <u>here</u>.

Wishing you happy reading and listening...

More on Courses and Publishing

I've included these articles as the have unique viewpoints and actionable How-To's you can use to get maximal leverage out of your content.

I haven't updated them with the title article for this book, as that was a recent breakthrough and a seismic shift in book production.

Instead, they are additional views on the broader approach to producing and marketing your book-type content. These views you may find controversial. But if you look up what I'm saying here, you'll also find they are grounded in studying the successful authors to see how their own production has scaled.

You'll also see that each has its own audio linked. As well, the original links to various downloads have been kept (in the PDF and ebook versions.)

The core ideas here to these articles are few:

Your book is an idea container.

You can work from a book to a course, or backwards, or any approach in between. As in card games, play from your strong suit.

Publish to Multiple Eyeballs

You want to leverage your content in all possible formats, on all possible marketplaces. This diversifies you income streams and gives the reader/viewer/listener exactly the type of content they most want. Meanwhile, these marketplaces are marketing your book to their particular users. They win, your audience wins, and your bank account wins.

Publish a Deep Backbench

As in any sports, having a lot of players is essential. As many as possible means you can read that many more readers. Also, if they liked one of your books, they'll probably buy others.

And a few other ideas remain...

As of this writing, there are a few more subjects to take up.

- **Course Building For Authors** (The full how-to and breakdown.)
- **Affiliate Income for Authors**
- **Promotion and Copywriting For Authors**
- **The Business Model for Indie Publishing**

These will be published as I get that research completed.

You can see from this current approach that these will become courses in order to produce the books. But they will probably start out as podcasts first, so be sure to follow and subscribe to Selling Your Book Online.

Meanwhile, here's some more educational, entertaining, and hopefully inspiring articles for your study...

How to Resolve and Expand Your Audience Out Of Trust

(<u>Listen to this audio here.</u>)

The core value any online commerce runs on is trust.

Yet business schools don't teach this. They are instead given all sorts of models to use which take them away from why they are there to begin with.

A business is a ongoing exchange of valuable services and/or products – usually in return for that commodity called money. (But not always.)

The major problem that business courses and online training have is that they are so busy teaching the How's that they forget the Why's.

Look at that definition above. It's all *continuing exchange of value.*

That all has to happen in an atmosphere of *trust.* The seller has to trust the buyer and vice-versa. These are age-old principles, which tend to help us understand how it's done these days in digital-everything.

The reverse of this is a scam, where whatever is promised is only partially delivered. (See my "<u>Get Your Self Scam Free</u>" for more details of this.)

There is no decent physical model to explain what happens in marketing.

Perhaps the stupidest or laziest one is calling it a "funnel." That implies once people enter at the top, they eventually move down to the bottom and out.

This model doesn't deal with the fact that people are leaving all the time because they don't want or can't trust the person or group they are dealing with.

A better model is a set of concentric circles. People start on the outside edge and gravitate toward the center as you improve your relationships with them.

The ideal flow of customers – and customers implies they are following a custom, or cultural habit – goes from less trust toward greater. Your clients come very closely in to you, and what you do, to absorb everything possible. When they've achieved the highest pinnacle of what you can offer, then they do one of three things:

1. They move on to another mentor, or

2. They go back through the material from the start, or

3. They become evangelists for your material and bring new customers to you.

The Usual Suspects, the Usual Lies

Recently, I laid out how the Social Media has been pushed as the latest Shiny Object. I wasn't so complimentary about it, as it was described as "<u>Revenge of the Social Media Zombies.</u>"

Social Media, and even book distributors (like Amazon) are on that outer ring. People come and go, they even buy your books and you have no clue who they are or what they did for you.

That outer ring isn't worth much of your time to deal with, as there are no reliable ways to build trust. You cast a wide net of content out there, and invite them closer in to you.

Next in would be to get them as subscribers to one of your feeds, so they could get your particular brand of content on a regular basis. This is your blog and podcast. Blogs are less reliable as most people don't know how to simply subscribe to a feed and get your data regularly, so podcasts are further in.

The next closer ring is an opt-in email subscription, where they can get a regular newsletter from you. Here is where you can build your relationships more closely. At any time, you can communicate directly to individuals, or vice-versa, and improve your mutual trust.

Even closer in would be a membership, where they have to log-in to get your special content. Here you are able to track their interests more closely, and find out what people are clicking on within your own site.

Memberships don't have to be paid, and it is probably best to have a free one at the outset. They do have to sign in and take that extra step to get your material. They have to demonstrate a little more trust. And you reward that with exclusive value.

From here on in, and closer, you'll be able to offer tailor-made products to them. With their feedback, you can carefully improve the value of the content they are looking for. And, if this content is good enough, they'll pay you for it.

Courses start showing up here. Especially when delivered with a Learning Management System (LMS). You can then open a course up which is delivered on demand, not on a time schedule. People can progress at their own pace, and you can send them tailor-made emails to encourage and debug them.

And this is where it gets quite interesting. Because the trust becomes mutual.

As the trust increases, you can offer ever-greater value, and your clients will start to exchange with you more frequently and in greater volume (you can set and get higher payments.)

Errors, Mistakes, and Misdirections

Most of the misdirections which are being spread ignore this trust factor.

For authors, this can be very confusing. Amazon pays for sales, but doesn't build trust. Your buyers are completely anonymous. And you probably know more about your reviewers (especially the trolls) than you do about your buyers.

Like Social Media, there is tons of "free" advice about how to get sales on Amazon. A lot of it is spread by Amazon itself, who wants you to only sell on their platform.

Let me repeat – Amazon is the *outer* ring of trust. Right out there with strangers giving you odd looks.

Here's how you use Social Media – post your content with invitations to join your mailing list. "Interaction" (like resistance to the Star Trek's Borg) is futile. Always syndicate to as many social networks as possible.

Here's how you use Amazon and all ebook distributors – post your content with invitations to join your mailing list. Never respond to reviews. Always publish to as many distributor platforms, in as many formats as possible. Always. Because they each have different audiences.

Do you see the similarities?

You don't spend a lot of your valuable time where you'll have nothing to show for it.

You can't build lasting relationships by "interacting" on either social networks or book distributors.

The one exception – perhaps – is to run something like a private Facebook group by invitation only. That is tricky, though, since that platform can shut you down at any time, just as the book distributors can cancel your account at any time (like Google Play has done to many Indie publishers.)

Ideally, you'd run a personal forum on your own site if you want to interact with people on that level. Like social media, it depends on how valuable your time is (as in "what should you be writing or editing right now?") You can get a return of money for monetary investments, you'll never be able to get time back for time spent. *Always invest money. Always spend time wisely.*

This model tells you to spend most of your time building relationships with those closest to you. By giving them private and exclusive special offers, they'll help you with reviews on Amazon and sending out tweets, plusses, and likes on your behalf. Those can attract attention and get people closer in.

But some percentage of your time needs to be spent on the middle ground as well. Guest blogging, and being a podcast guest are the ways you can build your audience by interacting with other's audiences.

In these, that existing audience is given the opportunity to join your inner circles. They trust the site you are appearing on, and can start building trust in you. Appearing as a guest takes more time than simply doing your own thing – but the investment pays off better.

Again, here's the breakdown:

Outer circles:

social media, book distributors
– syndicate content with offers to join your inner circles.

Middle Circles:

blogs, podcasts
– deliver regular, valuable content with offers to join, as well as appearing as guest (also with offers to join.)

Inner Circles:

free memberships, email subscription, private forums, free courses
– give them more valuable content and invest in relationship building with offers to purchase. These can start inviting others to join.

Closest circles:

paid memberships, paid courses, coaching
– this is very intensive relationship building. These can become your evangelists.

– – – –

I hope you've now started examining and discarding what you've been told about sales funnels and all the conventional wisdom around them. I know that this was a tough slog for years for myself and others, as there is just so much untested silliness being foisted off as Gospel these days.

Do test everything I say for yourself. Don't assume it's useful until you've tested it for yourself.

All this article is about is to lay out a common sense approach to timeless natural commerce principles.

As you uncover more of these natural principles for yourself, you should speed up your own progress toward the goals you've set.

4 Simple Author Models to Use For Your Ultimate Success

(Listen to the audio of this chapter here.)

Some of these are known, some can be observed. At least one isn't obvious at all. That last one only came up recently in trying to explain some mystery successes I'd heard about. But we'll get to that shortly.

There are four ways to be an exceptional success as an author:

1. Tap into an eternal desire with a book that is good enough to gain adoration. Doesn't have to be perfect. You've made a classic.
2. Promote yourself with advertising that raises your books to classic level. Expensive. Takes your whole life, if you aren't extremely smart about it.
3. Be prolific your whole life through and write in many varied genres. Produce your work in so many forms that your best become classics.
4. Wait until the time is right.

None of these can be faked. The *first* is often by accident, and is the first (and usually only) book the author ever publishes. If there are others, they are unlikely to succeed as well, since the first was an inspired stroke of lightning (that never strikes the same place twice.) You see this in J.D. Salinger, Margaret Mitchell, Anna Sewell.

Funny enough, only the *second* requires a great deal of advertising or remarkable marketing to make it happen. This is the most common approach these days. Grahl, Morkes, Dawson, Stephenson, and others are our current crop.

The *third* gains by sheer brute force of will and rivers of sweat-equity. That set knows all about publishing and has worked out what people want and how to best serve them. They serve humanity by using the long tail. Charles Dickens was one of these. Isaac Asimov another.

The *final one* is where the other three start. The author who starts only when the time is right. And otherwise makes their way through this world with a Day Job. We know who we are.

Each of these four types have their "platform" in place, even if they don't know it.

The one-shot-wonder taps into a wide audience with that classic and rules thereafter. There is enough sales to that book that they can live off residuals (or reinvest them) thereafter.

The second is constantly promoting to his audience in order to keep them. They move into and out of various forms to be worthy of following. Once they quit advertising, their books slowly dwindle down in sales. The promotion is what keeps their audience following them.

The third is alway paddling away in their river of interest, always finding more to write about and loving their lifestyle. By sheer volume, some of their stories become great hits. Others sell well. Some don't sell. But there is always another story after that last one. If they are promoted, someone else is doing it as part of their team. Someone else running their marketing. Because they are too busy writing and inventing and describing in order to pay much attention to the world at large.

The fourth has an invisible audience who is waiting.

Each serves humanity. Each has their own way to do so.

Their story of success in each case is different. The story of the first one is enigmatic and cannot be explained easily.

The story of the second one is explained too much, as they constantly are promoting themselves and selling courses on how to do it as well as they did.

The third will tell people to simply write what they are interested in (and their market will buy) and to read other authors in order to improve their own style.

The fourth reads all about the other authors and buys their books, courses, and audio.

The first and third are not believed. People spend a great deal of money in the second, but learn to write no better and have no more particular success than any of the three types. The fourth generally they keep their day job, as they are always buying courses and not doing the writing they want and have a need to do – yet.

The first are the real leaders, and they never particularly wanted to be.

The second are the following-followers. They don't really listen to their intuition to be as good as the first one. And don't have enough persistence to be a dogged success as the third. They live well as long as they keep finding stuff to promote to their audience to keep them interested.

The third lives well and independently, because their content can be consumed by multiple audiences. If their marketer is also a good manager, they live a comfortable life.

The fourth live as good a life as they work for others.

Amazon, and other book outlets fund the first three well. The fourth is part of that funding effort.

It's your choice which you will be, even though most people think they can't be one of the first, and don't want to "work as hard" as the third. So they either crack the conventional wisdom of the second, or keep their day job until they buy enough courses and read enough great books to work it all out.

I've studied all four types and can tell you that any of them can by done by anyone. The first is mystic, the second is mechanical, the third is inspired, the fourth is where we all start out.

None is any easier than the other. The hardest might be the fourth type: those who won't just sit down and write the stories that come to them and so never get started at all. They keep their day jobs. (And, if they only saved 10% out of every single paycheck they got for 40 years, they'd be a millionaire on retirement and could live off the interest comfortably. That would also be a great time to write.)

No one tells any of these four how to succeed. They each count their success differently. Salinger and Mitchell relished their private lives. The business person with their single book and the speaking gigs and coaching deals, keeps promoting themselves and enjoying the respect. (Celebrities fit this mold.) The fairly anonymous authors who crank out tons of work under pen-names enjoy doing what they are doing and are well supported by their sales. The fourth has a decent job, and all the security that can go with it, as well as all the entertainment it can buy.

All are authors in their own right.

Mark Twain in his "Letters From the Earth" described seeing a line of the greatest generals in history. At the head was someone dressed as a common farmer. The explanation for the obvious question, "Well, he just never got around to generalling."

You are an author first in your own mind. The rest of it depends on what actions you take.

This study started out because the collection of material on the how-to's of authorship was mostly filled with the stories of people who had made it big by promoting their few books and then bridging off into courses and affiliate sales. Also in this category were entrepreneurs who published only a single book and then make a living with that (and brand extensions.) This huge category seemed to be all there was. And the conventional wisdom was that an author needed to learn to sell and promote and give talks and so on. (Meanwhile, the authors themselves said they disliked having to do this, and would rather just be writing.)

That huge amount of data didn't explain the one-hit wonders. (Nothing really seems to, except metaphysics. This was their time and they took it.)

Meanwhile, my own route was publishing everything I could lay my hands on in addition to my own written works. Some sold, some didn't. A few did really well. But I was able to get my financial freedom enough to simply do research. The more I researched and published, the better I did financially. On the fringes, I started collecting other stories of people who were making six-figures from just writing what they felt like and what people were interested in buying. A lot of these stories are in Geoff Shaw's "Kindling" course and his Facebook group.

The most disregarded has been the author who just "hasn't gotten around to it." There is absolutely nothing wrong with this category, although some will beat themselves up because of being there. One day, they will move into one of the categories above, or they won't.

The point to any life is thoroughly enjoying what you are doing while you are doing it. *Joy is what we are really here for*. And the more joy you spread, the more you get back.

With that, my studies of the "how-to's" of authorship are complete. And thanks to the books I've published, I was able to afford all these courses. Digesting them will still take some time, and will wind up with other books for you to read. But I don't need buy any more courses or webinars or how-to manuals. I am going to write up what I've found, just to get it out of my head. After that, and probably at the same time, I'm going to find some more books to write, edit, publish, produce – all just for you, to spread the joy I've found.

My only advice to this is: *Have fun with your choices*. Choose to do those things you can enjoy.

Self-Publishing Secrets Every Author Should Know

(Listen to this audio here.)

I stumbled across these while researching and testing. I haven't seen them anywhere else, and they they are extremely practical ideas.

First, You Have to Change Your Thinking

1. **Authors are Producers.** They generate "books-as-containers," creating all possible versions of that title. Leverage is in multiple versions, as well as a multiple titles in a series. That makes the income generate exponentially rather than linearly.

2. **The non-fiction writer should work from the <u>course</u> backward**s, enabling the audience to help edit and build the experience. (I'll go over courses as another episode. This note is to tell you what the fastest, and most profitable way to build your list.)

3. **The author-producer doesn't "sell."** They offer audience-experiences to explore. Descriptions and landing pages need to be written to draw the viewer/reader/listener into the story that title affords. It's more fishing than anything else – cast a wide net and hook the audience by drawing them in by their own participation, interest, and trust. That audience wants to have a novel experience. The author-producer supplies it.

Second, Have a Smart Sequence of Producing Your Titles.

Begin with the end in mind.

The whole point to publishing is to leverage every piece of content you create to earn you the most possible income.

Most authors have this completely wrong.

First conventional thought: I'll write a great book and make millions. Sorry. Most writers don't make more than $500 a year, with 3,000 sales for the life of the book.

Second conventional thought: I'll write a series of books, give the first one away, and make millions. Sorry. While that can give you regular income, it doesn't take you to the tipping point.

Third conventional thought: I'll use social media to develop a following and get them to buy my books. Sorry. Especially these days, less than 10 percent of your "following" will ever see your posts.

If you study the successful authors, you'll find a different approach. It's not obvious, but it works.

Yes, they all write lots of books. But that's just the beginning.

a) They get readers to opt-in to their mailing list. Lead Magnets in every book, front and back.

b) Out of that mailing list, they recruit reviewers ("ambassadors") who get advanced copies and scour for errors. Those ambassadors are then asked to leave an honest review when the book goes live.

c) They alert that entire list to the pre-order offer, to the low-intro-price offer, and before the price goes up.

d) They rinse-repeat with all subsequent books.

e) They meanwhile run FB ads to spike book sales, so Amazon will push it through their promotions.

Now, even less obvious:

f) They sell everywhere else in addition to Amazon, and run FB ads for iTunes users to buy the book there, also Kobo gets a similar treatment. (Haven't heard anyone doing this for Nook...)

g) They get the book recorded and published as an audiobook.

h) They publish the paperback and hardback versions.

i) They get translations and publish those as well, or sell the foreign rights to someone who will.

j) They get paid speaking gigs.

The real hidden options, particularly for non-fiction authors:

k) They make courses out of the book series.

Why this works

If you're just writing more books, it can only increase your sales linearly. Practically, the earlier books in any series will tend to downtrend in sales as later ones come out and the market has mostly read your books. That also dampens sales overall. FB ads, particularly for box sets, tends to spice things up a bit.

If you are offering more versions of your books, you get into different reading audiences. You now have more books in series in front of multiple audiences. Popular books will tend to reinforce each other (especially on Amazon where all versions are sold.)

If your books are popular in multiple areas, then the sales aggregate more exponentially

Why courses?

There is a progression of content from digital text to printed text, to audio, to video, to courses. Courses are the container for all versions of the content you produced originally as an ebook.

Courses have more ways they can be distributed. While there are four main book distributors, courses can be offered on about 15 or more distributors in various formats. Obviously, more people are looking for digital packages of materials than just a single digital version. People have more ways of learning than just reading on their smartphone.

The general principle of promotion is to put your offer in front of as many different audiences as possible – with their permission.

The multiple eyeballs theorem confirms this, but goes further to say you need to be putting it out there in as many formats as possible as well. While you probably won't sell many videos on YouTube, you can get links to your course page where they can buy a course with that video in it.

Begin with the course in mind.

- The best way to write a book is to get the audience to help you with it.

- The best way to produce a course is to get the students to help you compile it.

- The best way to run an FB ad promotion is to a paid service or product where the sales will cover your advertising costs.

You can see where this is going: Announce a course before you build it, run ads to get people to buy it, and then use their feedback to build the course materials as they start taking it.

Before that, you have other steps.

0) Do set up the course with its outline and introduction page – don't put any content on it yet.

1) Do your homework and write the sales page. Create several with different course names. Use the one that converts the best.

2) Use that sales page and course name to create the introduction to the course. Short video, PDF transcript, downloadable audio.

3) Create the prelaunch videos that lay out what is going to be in the course. Set these up in a sequence and track

opens. Run your FB ads into this landing page and autoresponder sequence.

4) Start building out the course, by making one lesson live and with open-ended survey questions that have to be answered before the next lesson opens. (Once you've completed the course and ran enough students through it, you can take the surveys down.)

5) Start building your next course in the series. Survey your students for what they want before you start anything.

6) Rinse-repeat – until you have courses for all the books you've written.

6a) This is also the way you write the books based on what you taught in the course, which is simpler. Just start with a problem area and the known solutions. Give them your own particular take on it and start from there with your FB ads.

Authors should produce courses in order to write the textbooks.

They should start with courses and build their base from there.

Your text, audio, and graphics will all be ready at the same time. Practically, you'll be able to publish your books, audiobooks, and bundles while the course is being built. These book-versions will then each be emissaries for your course and bring you more students.

That is the new top-level strategy for non-fiction authors.

Have fun with this.

The Beginner's Book Launch – How to Survive and Prosper

<u>(Listen to this audio here.)</u>

It's time I collated all the material on book launches to sort out how to do this and give myself a plan I can follow.

The biggest problem with book launches is that they are either undocumented at the beginning stages, or don't really tell what they did. There's this gap between a person who starts writing books, and suddenly there's a person with several books who has a huge list and can use that list to launch every new book to a big success.

So I went back over all the material I've collected over the years having anything to do with launches. Most of it sucked, as usual. Either it wasn't real, or it was incomplete like above. Some was a mix – they filled in what they didn't know with conjecture. Like mortar used between bricks shouldn't be used to fill in the spot where a brick should be.

If you already have a list

Good for you.

In that case:

> 1) Find which ones want to be your reviewers. Segment these out and send them proofed copies of your book before you publish for their honest review and comments. Adjust the book based on what they tell you – or not. Part of the deal is that they should give your book honest reviews when it comes out.

> 2) Set your book up for pre-sales on Amazon (and everywhere else that enables this) and hit the podcast circuit to tell them about it.

3) When the book goes live, tell your list. Price it at .99 for the first five days or a week.

4) When you're price is ready to go up to normal, you then remind your list again.

5) Once your price is where you want it, then you get back to finishing off your next book.

That is the normal launch for an established author. It primes the pump for Amazon and if it's successful enough, they'll start promoting your book for you. Mark Dawson and other authors will also run Facebook Ads to also accelerate the process, but Dawson usually only runs these on higher-priced sets where the sales income will pay for the ad costs. (Take his course if you can. Save everything to your hard drive so you can review it as much as you want.)

What most authors without a list do:

1) Publish the book at full price.

2) Hope.

3) Start writing their next one.

What most authors do to get a list:

Blog when they should be writing. (Of course you can also just convert your blog into a book afterwards.) The bribes and "content upgrades" you offer can be used as incentives for people to join your list. Eventually (years later) you have a decent sized list – providing you've then started relationships with them, such as maintaining a regular newsletter and also weeding out those who never open emails after that first one.

The next thing they do is to guest blog, which gets their content in front of other audiences, so they'll join yours.

Once you have a list, then you can do the first approach, which is most common.

Some will do the second and get some books out there, and then move to the first approach when they have enough of a list to make a difference.

Research shows a third route.

I did find that in general, the most routinely successful "launchers" used Jeff Walker's Product Launch Formula, or something derived from it. Of interest to us is his "seed" launch, where you don't really have a product to start with. By including your audience into your launch, you can then build your product as the audience goes through it.

Another datum showed up over and over that you really only want to publish once you have at least three books ready to go. (More on this point below.)

As well, you want to include your audience in writing your books – which is nearly impossible without having an audience in the form of a list.

Recent research on courses shows that this is the most likely candidate to be successful in list building, especially for non-fiction authors.

Why ?

> 1) Walker's "seed" launches have a record of building lists full of people who buy things.

> 2) You get instant reviews from everyone who participates.

> 3) Buyers tend to work to get their "money's worth" and so will remain involved.

> 4) Courses pitch your books, and allow you to revise your books as well.

> 5) Courses help solve list building, relationship building, and income building.

> 6) People will buy an expensive course when they won't buy a cheap ebook.

What I'm saying here is that doing a launch of a course plus your books looks to be the best way an unknown author can get started.

What makes up a seed launch: step by step

There are some steps which are common to all marketing which have to be included. Walker covers these slightly, but they are basic enough to be mentioned.

I. Pre-pre-launch

1. Who is your buyer?

You want to know about your ideal customer. This is an avatar, a fleshed-out concept. When you write, when you market, you do it all to one person. Just as when you are on a podcast – the best ones you listen to seem like they are talking directly to you. The best books you read are written just for you.

2. What problem are you solving for your buyer?

This is obviously pointed toward non-fiction authors. (Fiction authors have the problems of plot, character, and genre.)

Of course, you can study the forums to find these. While this is pushed by these "overnight success from Kindle" scam-authors, it's a true datum. You will also find out what kind of terms they are using. It's important to talk to them in the language they use. Just search for "

[problem area]

+ forum"

You pick the problem area by something that interests you which you have had to find answers for or can't find answers for. (Like how this podcast was started.)

3. Find your own voice.

Most people have been trained from birth to lie to themselves and everyone around them. They have never been taught to simply appreciate who they are and what they can contribute to this world. Those that have usually don't talk about the experience of making the shift from trying to please everyone to just having and following a basic purpose or goal. When you talk about people like Edison, Ford, Franklin, Steve Jobs, Einstein, Elon Musk, Bill Gates – these people succeeded in spite of everyone around them. That's usually attribted to being simply brilliant and genius and all that. Actually, it's because they were almost brutally honest with themselves.

I prefer to study successful people who studied successful people and distill what they did and how they act into a short list of common principles. Joe Pulizzi did this recently with his book "Content Inc." In that book, he lists 6 principles that all the successful businesses he studied used to get that way. One of these was what he called "Content Tilt." Every successful individual and business used what they knew and what they were interested in order to narrow down to a niche they could succeed in. Pulizzi talks about a "Chicken Whisperer" who couldn't find data on how to raise chickens in your back yard. When he visited forums, he found out a lot of people were out there just like him. So he used the answers he was finding and set up a site and products to help those people. And became an internationally known expert as a result (and also enjoyed nice profits.)

You have to take what you already know how to do (make a list) and compare this to what you are fascinated by (make a second list). You'll find crossovers here and the best combination will give you your particular voice.

In this podcast, I give you suggestions on how you can make a living self-publishing. Each one is designed around the idea that you start from scratch with nothing but a computer and an Internet link. I also give it to you without fluff and sugar-coating. But that is my approach to this stuff. Writing is easy for me, so is researching. But marketing books has to be done, so I write about the problems I run into and the solutions I find. That's my voice.

What's your voice?

When you know who you are talking to, what they want to solve, and how you can talk to them about it, then you are ready to being to start.

II. Pre-Launch

The conventional prelaunch means getting enough people into the pilot so that you can get feedback. Walker's first seed launch had 6 buying customers and he "comped" another 24 people into the course so that he had enough interested people to get it rolling. (He got those 6 people by speaking at a conference.)

But he recommends getting at least that many people onto your list and into that launch.

There's a bunch of hooey that happens around here that says go out to social media and connect with people so they get interested in being an early adopter and reviewer for you. Even Jeff Walker says on one of his videos that it's really dead-simple to get between 50 and 100 email subscribers by going out to social media. But he doesn't tell you how. (Thanks, Jeff.) Another "authority" who sells courses on how to get thousands onto your list, at least tells you to use the old MLM trick of contacting 100 of your friends and asking them to join your list.

The problem with this is that they aren't really your audience. They are a start, and that's it. It's not certain that this will even prime your pump.

Right now, the best course of action – although you probably don't want to hear it – is to run Facebook Ads to get course buy-in.

This is my route right now. This is a test of my own dogfood. This podcast is just saying that all these points have tended to show up at the same time and point in this direction.

I've bought Mark Dawson's FB ads course. And finished most of it. The rest now has a reason to get completed, as well as a probable restudy of anything I still have a question on. (You find his intro videos elsewhere on the web, where they explain a great deal of the basics.) Or you could get a Perry Marshall book on it.

So: set up your basics course somewhere (Teachable or Thinkific are free to get started, Udemy will keep your price at $50 or less.) Don't put much up other than a representative landing page with good art, and the outline, plus maybe the first lesson. Set your price at something it will be worth by the time you finish it – and include a discount for being part of the pilot (with lifetime access.)

Now start building your prelaunch sequence.

You'll need four videos which build excitement, per the usual "sideways sales letter" that Walker lays out. You'll also need to create downloads (content upgrades) as bonus gifts so people can review your material and test it for themselves.

You then create the emails which will introduce and keep the audience excited through the sequence. Walker's full course goes into this in more details with the "triggers" and "hooks" he uses to pull everything off.

I'll be hosting this on my own site, as it's built on Rainmaker and allows all this automation to be built in. The course itself is also hosted on my own site with Rainmaker's LMS.

You can do all the above with a decent autoresponder service and virtually any of the course providers I've listed. And it shouldn't cost you more than sweat equity if you've already invested in a podcast mic and set up (less than $100.)

III. Launch

Your actual launch date is built into the autoresponder sequence. The course will accept buy-ins at any point, you just have to tell them where to find it. But then you can shut off new students on the date you set in order to build anticipation for the next launch.

If this is all you want to do, you can simply re-launch this course several times a year to generate income in spikes. Each launch is better than the last as you come out with new versions.

The Breakdown of Income From a New Course

This approach seems the most sensible, as every ring of that hub-and-spoke marketing can get its chance at making income for you, or at least being lead generators.

> 1. Every lesson has a short-read ebook, thin paperback, podcast, powerpoint, and video.

> 2. eBooks and paperbacks sold on the various book distributors. Podcasts are delivered one per week with the course sponsoring them. Powerpoints are posted on Slideshare for SEO purposes – with ads for that course. Videos (with extra ads inserted for the course, as well as links) are posted to YouTube.

> 3. Your course is also promoted on the marketplaces. Affiliate sales are also enabled.

The result should be tons of people to fill your list. Your new eBooks add to your deep backbench and your other books should start selling better. Your podcasts should produce leads, but also give you audio for the videos and a later audiobook. Your videos can produce leads. Together, all these parts increase your income as a course. And then you create a comprehensive book that can be sold as ebook or paperback (even deluxe dust cover hardback) through Amazon and everywhere else.

Evergreen Launch versus Time-limited.

Regular launches stick you to the clock, personally. You have deadlines to meet, and like a Kickstarter cycle (just another launch, actually) for a month, you are tied into making sure that this cycle goes well. It just depends on how well you promote it and get the "buzz" going.

But you're stuck to that clock.

I don't like that. My muses don't like that. Running a launch means having another J.O.B. to slave at.

Consider the option of an Evergreen launch. When someone opts in, they are given a link which starts a sequence of pre-scheduled content happening. You are creating a user experience that they can graduate from, or not.

All your material is still there – and you can get busy working up the course meanwhile, releasing parts of it and checking back for comments to correct what you have set there. For me, I'd take my current membership list and "comp" them all in just so I could get the feedback.

Once I'm done with that pre-launch sequence, I then move onto creating the course. I can then take the time needed to write other books that may be needed as part of the course. I no longer worry about selling the course itself, or having a spike and dive of my income. Meanwhile, I'm running FB ads to get people into the course, and watching the feedback on those ads. I can always take down the pre-scheduled prelaunch, or just close down the landing page which starts it. Then I could run a regular launch at any time.

This fits better for my lifestyle as I keep finding material that needs to be researched, or written and podcast for my audience. I'm not putting the rest of my life on hold until I can get back to it.

You see, a regular launch has the pre-launch, the launch, and the review. Then it has building the course itself and its own review. Only then (unless an emergency happens) do you get back to your regular schedule.

On the evergreen launch, while you are increasing your list and income, you don't have to put off anything else you want to do.

Sure, this is about a year's worth of work for the massive projects I'm planning. And as well, I'm going to be doing this for two courses at once. I still intend to continue regular publishing of classic public domain works as I can. (So don't try this at home without adult supervision.)

And it's taken this overlong podcast to sort all this out.

Hub and Spoke Marketing For Books

(Listen to this audio here.)

On tallying up all the distributors I've been able to find, one point emerged: *there are distributors at every level and for every version of your book, who want to promote your book for free.*

That is remarkable, as it shows you can get paid for every type of material you produce. In Internet Marketing, this has been called a "self-liquidating offer" and "funded proposal."

What is different in this approach is that other marketers have build audiences around their own marketplace to sell yours and other's products.

- When you have an ebook, there are: Amazon, iTunes, Kobo, Nook and some others.

- When you create paperbacks and hardbacks, you have CreateSpace (on Amazon) and Ingrams to all brick and mortar stores via Lulu. There is also the global Espresso Book Machine Network.

- With PDF's, you can sell them via Scribd, Lulu, and HummingbirdDM

- When you create audiobooks, you have: ACX/Audible, iAmplify, and now Authors Republic and Hummingbird Digital Media (who also do ebooks)

- When you have video-based courses, you have: Udemy and Open Sesame.

- With bundles of these digital goods, you have: BitTorrent, Small Business Trends Marketplace, Tradebit, JVZoo, MyCommerce, DigiResults, BlueSnap, Distribly.

Each of these will promote your materials for you and then send you the bulk of the profits. (And yes, all these are linked in the show notes, as well as a downloadable PDF.)

For all I've studied over the last 15 years about Internet Marketing, I've never seen it more possible to profit by creating a branded solution based on a single set of content.

Let's look at how this would happen.

(Links in the PDF download.)

1) Say you have three ebooks (the minimum any author could get away with publishing.) They could also be Public Domain, or rewritten PLR (private license rights) books.

On ebooks, the first is free, the second you give away for an email, and the third you sell, as well as the collection. All have Lead Magnets in them to get the readers onto your mailing list as a subscriber.

(In addition to having an autoresponder service, this considers that you have a site and your own domain with landing pages for each book that you can update with all the various sales links.)

2) Now you publish via CreateSpace and Lulu to create the paperbacks and hardback versions of these.

3) Next, you record the audio for these books and sell the audiobooks on Audible and Authors Republic, as well as offering them on your own site.

4) At this point, you can sell the collection on BitTorrent, as well as the other 7 digital product marketplaces. (And on some, you'll give a handsome affiliate commission for people selling them for you.)

5) The next logical action, particularly for non-fiction, is to create introductory courses for each book. These courses are put onto Udemy, Skillshare, and OpenSesame, and also on marketplaces such as Small Business Trends Marketplace.

6) Next is to create more expensive, full courses which can be hosted on your own site or taught via Teachable and/or Thinkific. If you built them originally on a non-marketplace provider, they can simply ported to Udemy, Skillshare, and OpenSesame as well. (And have them promoted as above.)

7) Through your newsletter, you've been keeping in touch with your audience as they progress through your trust circles and become ever closer. Meanwhile, you are recommending solutions (found in your materials) which they can use to become more entertained, educated, or inspired.

You are profiting at every stage. And can organize various sets of materials to create new products.

I didn't mention that you can use the audio to podcast, which would then promote your courses and materials – and could actually be created from the lessons themselves. Your show notes can have special discount coupons for the courses and ebooks.

See how this works? Fortunately, most of these either direct deposit or pay via PayPal, so you don't get tired out carrying sacks of money to the bank and then having to wait in line to deposit.

This is truly semi-automatic passive income which will last for years after you are gone.

This doesn't mean that's all you do. Obviously, running promotional ads and being a guest on other's podcasts will improve your sales. And those are necessary investments of time and money in order to improve income.

What do you do when you've gotten all this publishing done?

Start in with your next series of books – and turn them into all these versions. Your goal is to turn all your books into courses and everything in between.

This is the next phase for public domain publishing. No longer is it a problem in how you can get a few hundred PD works up and compete with everyone else at low, low prices.

- Research a problem area in a niche you are interested in.
- Find a collection of books that fill solve that niche problem.
- Edit them into professional shape.
- Improve their cover, description, and give them respectable prices (not the "race to the bottom" Amazon encourages.)
- Publish them as a series and a bundle.
- Publish the paperbacks and hardback editions.
- Record and publish the audiobooks.
- Create a podcast series based on those books which promote the other versions.
- Create a series of courses, an intro for the series, plus an intro and "master class" for each book.
- Promote all these materials.

Then research a new problem area – based on your audiences concerns – and produce a new series of books in this area. Rinse/repeat.

The other option, especially with your most popular courses, is to come out with post-grad course built on additional material that author referred to or a subsequent book of his. (Napoleon Hill, for instance, actually had three bestsellers, not just the one.)

You can also re-launch your original books and courses with the post-grad versions.

As you keep building new book series, audiobooks, and courses each year, you'll soon have a deep backbench of books which have their own related materials people can keep on buying.

And eventually, you have that publishing empire and hire a freelance publicist to keep everything raking in income hand over fist.

Just so you can keep finding more books to help people with their problems. And your biggest problem is finding who is worthy enough to inherit your publishing business to...

– – – – –

Click here to <u>Download List of Book Distributors – All Formats</u>

More Books in the Really Simple Writing & Publishing Series

Here's most all I know about writing and publishing up to this point. I've got four more books lined up to complete the missing subjects in this list below.

You can search for all these books on Amazon and all the major online book outlets and can even order printed editions through your nearby bookstore.

If you just click on the link in the front or back (or type it in) and opt-in to my mailing list, you can get them all for free as PDF's. The other versions you can also buy through links there.

Also, I'll be adding all my upcoming books on writing there, as well as some classics on grammar and word usage, and also some on storytelling.

These books are all available through Amazon or on my site as linked below.

Really Simple Writing & Publishing Series

(http://livesensical.com/book-series/publishing-and-writing/)

Really Simple Writing & Publishing

> Learn How to Write, Design, Format, Upload, and Sell Your Own Book for Low Cost or Free.

J'APE: Just Another Publicity Excuse

> How to Publish Your (Kindle) Book for Shameless Self-Promotion and Profit

Publish. Profit. Independence.

> How to Earn Extra Income and Financial Freedom by Publishing on Your Own

How to Write Less and Profit More

A Rich Adventure in Short Read Kindle Publishing

Writing Serial Fiction in the Real World

A Simple, Tongue-in-Cheek Guide to Writing and Publishing Episodic eBooks for Profit on Amazon (and Elsewhere.)

How to Help Librarians Fall in Love With Your Self-Published Book

...and Get More Sales When They Do.

Cracking the Kindle Sales Code

How to Search Engine Optimize Your Titles and Descriptions so Amazon Promotes Your Book and Recommends Buyers to You at No Cost

Your Kindle Booksales Blueprint

How to Break Out of the No-Sales Amazon Self-Publishing Basement and Routinely Start Getting Regular Passive Income From Your Kindle Booksales Without Added Expense or Tricks

Downloads For You

Here's the links to all the extra PDF's and other material I originally put up on the show notes for this podcast:

http://livesensical.com/podcast/selling-books-online/backwards-book-publishing-save-time-earn-work-less/

There you will find all these bonuses:

- **Audio**
- **Video**
- **Mindmap PDF**
- **Slides PDF**

Note : through this book, there are other links for additional downloads.

PS. If you want even more useful information, then click on the link in the Bonus section and sign up.

Bonus

Get No-Charge Access to Writing and Publishing Materials from Our Library Collection

Instant Access - Join Here

Click or type into your browser:

http://livesensical.com/go/writingbooks/

www.ingramcontent.com/pod-product-compliance
Lightning Source LLC
Chambersburg PA
CBHW021925170526
45157CB00005B/2190